ON THE TEAM

SOCCER

By Mason Burdick

Gareth Stevens
Publishing

Please visit our website, www.garethstevens.com. For a free color catalog of all our high-quality books, call toll free 1-800-542-2595 or fax 1-877-542-2596.

Library of Congress Cataloging-in-Publication Data

Burdick, Mason.
Soccer / Mason Burdick.
      p. cm. — (On the team)
Includes index.
ISBN 978-1-4339-6454-1 (pbk.)
ISBN 978-1-4339-6455-8 (6-pack)
ISBN 978-1-4339-6452-7 (library binding)
1. Soccer—Juvenile literature. I. Title.
GV943.25.B87 2012
796.334—dc23
                                        2011037282

First Edition

Published in 2012 by
Gareth Stevens Publishing
111 East 14th Street, Suite 349
New York, NY 10003

Copyright © 2012 Gareth Stevens Publishing

Designer: Michael J. Flynn
Editor: Greg Roza

Photo credits: Cover, p. 1 Stockbyte/Getty Images; p. 5 muzsy/Shutterstock.com; p. 6 Topical Press Agency/Hulton Archive/Getty Images; p. 13 iStockphoto.com; p. 14 Andreas Gradin/Shutterstock.com; pp. 17, 18, 21 Shutterstock.com; p. 20 Hector Mata/AFP/Getty Images.

Printed in the United States of America

CPSIA compliance information: Batch #CW12GS: For further information contact Gareth Stevens, New York, New York at 1-800-542-2595.

Contents

Words in the glossary appear in **bold** type the first time they are used in the text.

Get a Kick Out of Soccer!

Soccer requires skill, speed, and **stamina**. It also requires teamwork. Teammates pass a ball back and forth to keep it away from the other team. They score points by kicking the ball into a goal. They do it all without using their hands!

Soccer is one of the most popular team sports in the world. That might be because it doesn't take much to start a game—just a soccer ball and a group of friends.

THE COACH'S CORNER

In many countries, the game we call soccer is known as football. The Spanish call it "fútbol." In Germany, it's called "fussball."

Soccer players can't touch the ball with their hands, but they can use other parts of their body, such as their knees, chest, and even their head!

5

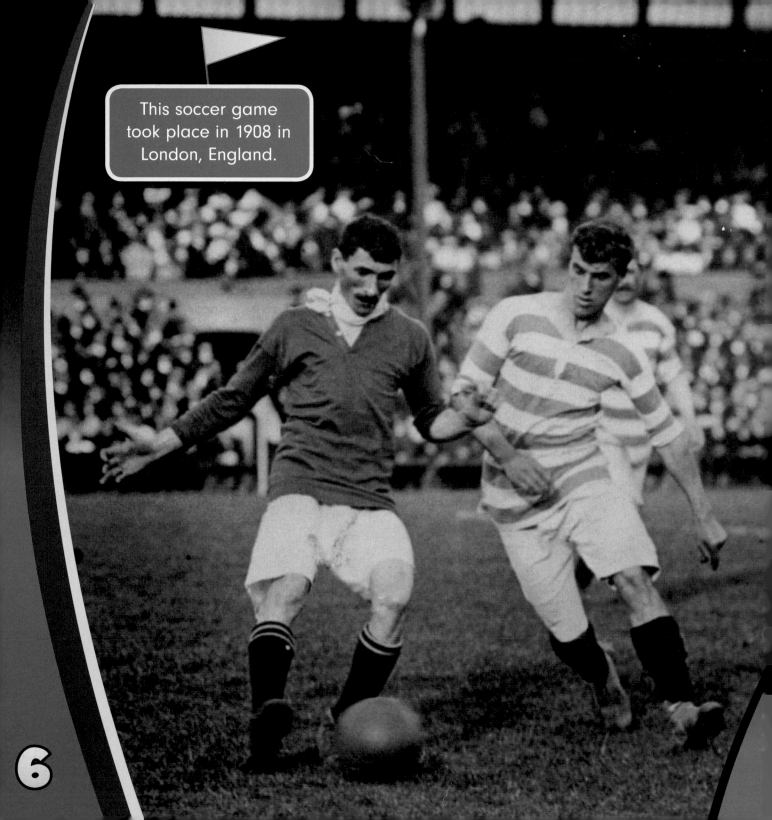

This soccer game took place in 1908 in London, England.

History of Soccer

People around the world have been playing games similar to soccer since ancient times. The game we're familiar with today began to take shape in England in 1863. That year, the first official rules were recorded. Soccer soon became popular in countries all over the world.

During the 1920s in the United States, soccer was as popular as football. Since then, the sport has had its ups and downs. Today, kids and teens play for school and town leagues across the country.

THE COACH'S CORNER

When soccer rules were first recorded, some people didn't like that players couldn't carry the ball in their hands. So, they created the game of rugby.

Hit the Field

Soccer is played on a grass field 100 yards (91 m) long and 60 yards (55 m) wide. At each end is a goal that measures 24 by 8 feet (7.3 by 2.4 m).

At the center of the field is a circle. Players on **offense** start there with the ball at the beginning of the game and after the other team scores a goal. The **defense** must stay out of this circle until the offense touches the ball.

end line

goal

goal area

penalty area

THE COACH'S CORNER

In front of each goal is a large rectangle called the penalty area. Breaking a rule inside the penalty area can give the other team a chance to score up close.

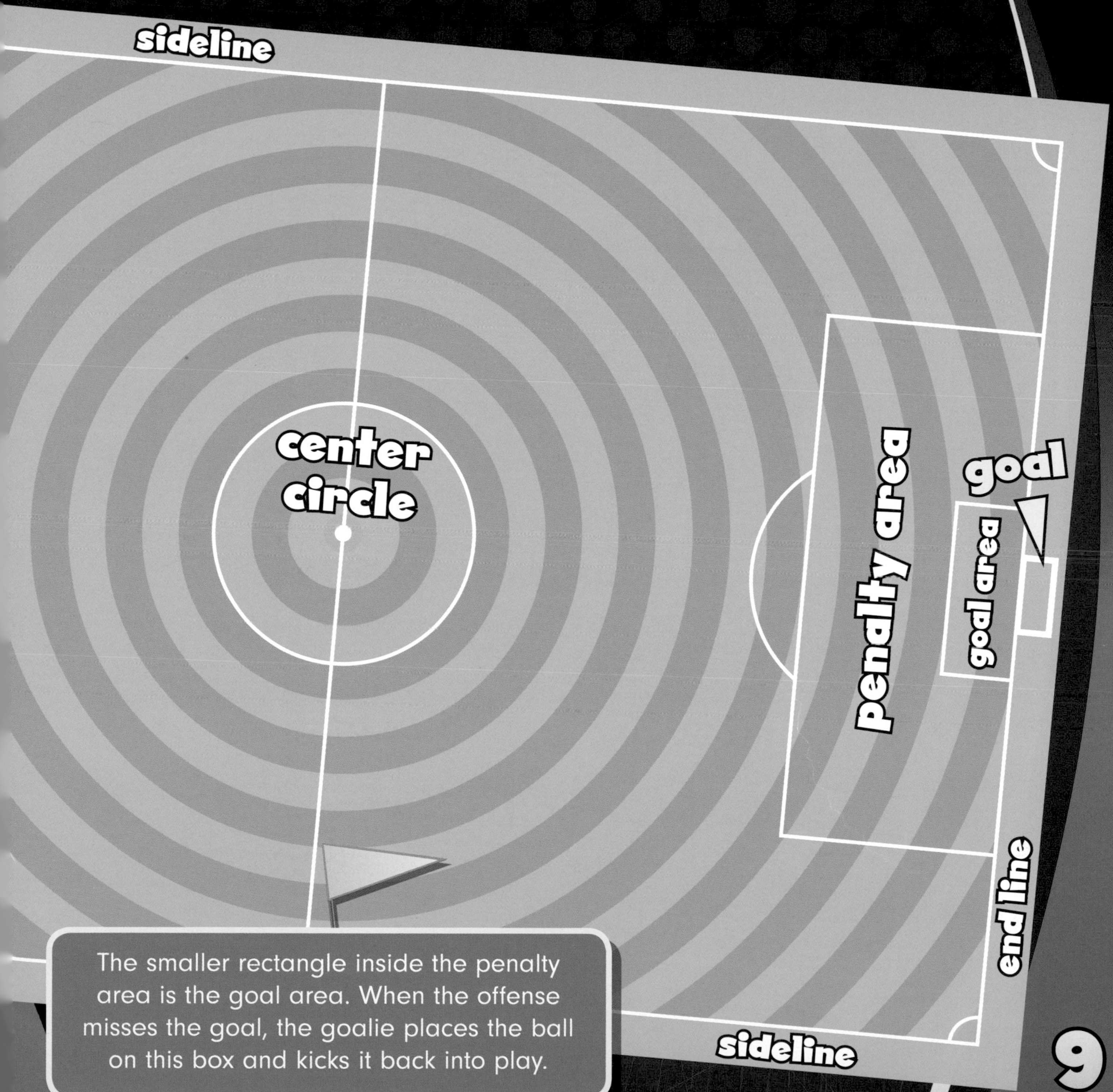

sideline

center
circle

penalty area

goal

goal area

end line

sideline

The smaller rectangle inside the penalty area is the goal area. When the offense misses the goal, the goalie places the ball on this box and kicks it back into play.

9

defender

forward

midfielder

defender

midfielder

forward

goalie

defender

midfielder

forward

defender

Regardless of their position, every player on a soccer team helps out on both offense and defense.

Soccer Positions

Each soccer team has 11 players on the field at a time. Goalies are the only players who can touch the ball with their hands.

Forwards play the farthest away from their own goalie. They're usually the best scorers on the team. Next come midfielders. They have to be fast because they switch between offense and defense often. Defenders play closest to their goalie and try to stop the other team from scoring.

THE COACH'S CORNER

A team's best forward is sometimes called the striker. A defender who's very good at stopping strikers is called the stopper.

11

Playing Offense

The team on offense is the one that controls the ball. Players try to get the ball into the other team's goal to score a point. All players on the team work together to get this done.

Offense often starts when the goalie throws or kicks the ball down the field. Players on offense get control of the ball and move toward the other team's goal. They pass the ball to each other to keep it away from the defense and to set up plays.

THE COACH'S CORNER

When the defense kicks the ball out of bounds near their own goalie, the offense gets a corner kick. This is a free kick from the corner of the field.

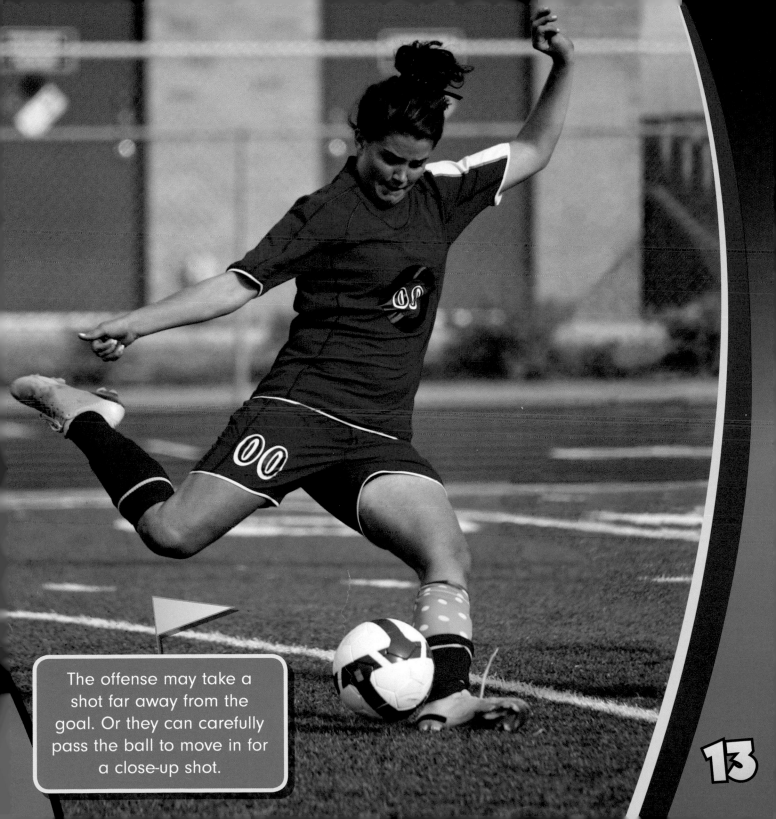

The offense may take a shot far away from the goal. Or they can carefully pass the ball to move in for a close-up shot.

13

When trying to tackle, players have to be careful not to hit another player with their arms or elbows.

14

Playing Defense

The defense tries to stop the offense from scoring. They run after the offensive players and try to take the ball from them. They can do this by **intercepting** a pass.

Defenders must be good at tackling. Unlike in football, soccer defenders don't pull other players to the ground when tackling. Instead, they use their feet to take the ball away from the offense. A defender must be careful not to trip the other player or they'll get a penalty.

THE COACH'S CORNER

During a slide tackle, the defender slides in front of another player and takes the ball away. Slide tackles can be very exciting, but also very dangerous.

Playing Goalie

The goalie guards their team's goal and tries to stop the other team from scoring. Goalies can use their hands to catch the ball or punch it away from the goal. Once they have the ball, goalies can roll, throw, or kick it to teammates.

The goalie is the last line of defense. Goalies must be quick and strong to stop a running forward who's about to score. They also help set up plays by shouting directions to their teammates.

THE COACH'S CORNER

Goalies often wear uniforms that are different from the uniforms other players wear. They wear long pants and shirts. They also wear thick gloves.

Goalies sometimes need to make diving saves!

Soccer **referees** use cards to announce penalties. A yellow card is a warning. A player who gets a red card must leave the game.

Fouls and Penalties

Soccer has a lot of rules. Breaking a rule gives the other team an advantage. A team might get a free kick. This gives the kicking team time to set up a play and get in position to score.

Fouls inside the penalty area can result in penalty kicks. The referee places the ball 12 yards (11 m) away from the goal. Only the goalie can try to stop a penalty kick. Penalty kicks usually result in a goal.

THE COACH'S CORNER

Most soccer games have a main referee and two assistant referees.

The World Cup

Soccer is a team sport that kids all over the world enjoy. Some play it on a school field. Some play it on a dirt lot. Some even play in a parking lot or in the streets.

Wherever it's played, soccer is one of the world's most popular sports. Many countries, including the United States, have **professional** leagues. The best players get to play for their country once every 4 years in the World Cup. Winning the World Cup is the greatest honor a soccer team can earn.

As They Say in Soccer...

back	a defender
center	a forward who plays in the middle of a line
halfback	a midfielder
keeper	the goalie, or goalkeeper
stopper	a defender who's good at stopping strikers
striker	the best scorer on a team
sweeper	a defender who plays behind the other defenders, close to their own goalie
throw-in	to throw the ball back into play when the other team kicks it out of bounds. This is the only time a player other than the goalie can touch the ball with their hands.
winger	a forward who plays on the end of a line

Glossary

defense: the team trying to stop the other team from scoring

intercept: to take control of a pass that was meant for a player on the other team

offense: the team trying to score

penalty: a loss for breaking a rule

professional: earning money from an activity that many people do for fun

referee: an official who makes sure players follow the rules

stamina: the strength needed to do something a long time

For More Information

Books

Crisfield, Deborah W. *The Everything Kids' Soccer Book: Rules, Techniques, and More About Your Favorite Sport!* Avon, MA: Adams Media, 2009.

Hornby, Hugh. *Soccer.* New York, NY: DK Publishing, 2010.

Websites

Soccer Fans Info
www.soccer-fans-info.com
Learn more about soccer, including its history, famous players, rules, and much more.

U.S. Soccer
www.ussoccer.com
Keep on top of the latest news about the national teams of the United States.

Index